XTREME PETS
FISH

BY S.L. HAMILTON

Visit us at
www.abdopublishing.com

Published by ABDO Publishing Company, PO Box 398166, Minneapolis, MN 55439.
Copyright ©2014 by Abdo Consulting Group, Inc. International copyrights reserved in all
countries. No part of this book may be reproduced in any form without written permission
from the publisher. A&D Xtreme™ is a trademark and logo of ABDO Publishing Company.

Printed in the United States of America, North Mankato, Minnesota.
042013
092013

PRINTED ON RECYCLED PAPER

Editor: John Hamilton
Graphic Design: Sue Hamilton
Cover Design: Sue Hamilton
Cover Photo: Getty Images
Interior Photos: AP-pg 26; Corbis-pgs 4-5, 8-9, 20-21 & 24-25; Dreamstime-pgs 6-7, 14-15
& 28-29; Getty Images-pgs 16-17; Glow Images-pgs 1 & 12-13; Science Source-pgs 10-11;
Thinkstock-pgs 2-3, 18-19, 22-23, 26-27, 30-31 & 32.

ABDO Booklinks
Web sites about Xtreme Pets are featured on our Book Links pages. These links are routinely
monitored and updated to provide the most current information available.
Web site: www.abdopublishing.com

Library of Congress Control Number: 2013931672

Cataloging-in-Publication Data

Hamilton, Sue.
   Fish / Sue Hamilton.
     p. cm. -- (Xtreme pets)
   ISBN 978-1-61783-973-3
   1. Fishes--Juvenile literature. 2. Pets--Juvenile literature.   I. Title.
   597--dc23

                                                            2013931672

CONTENTS

XTREME PETS: FISH

Pet fish bring a sense of calmness and color to a room. People enjoy keeping freshwater or saltwater tanks. Some owners have large ponds for their pet fish.

Bettas, also known as Siamese fighting fish, are popular freshwater tank fish.

XTREME FACT– A person who keeps fish in an aquarium is known as an "aquarist."

Fish require care and an understanding of their needs. Many pet fish come to know their owners. Some fish can even be taught tricks. All are fun to watch!

FRESHWATER FISH

Freshwater fish come from water sources with little amounts of salt, such as lakes and rivers. Owners who maintain freshwater aquariums have their choice of many unusual pets.

PIRANHA

Piranha are freshwater fish from South America. Although they are famous as vicious sharp-toothed fish, they are actually omnivores, eating both plants and meat. Red-bellied piranha may grow to a length of 8-10 inches (20-25 cm). They may live for 4 to 10 years. Piranha prefer a large tank with many hiding places.

Red-Bellied Piranha

XTREME FACT– Piranha teeth have been used to make tools and weapons.

AROWANAS

rowanas are one of the most expensive freshwater tank fish. Rare species may cost as much as $2,000-5,000. Many people think these beautiful and graceful fish bring luck to their owners. Arowanas grow as big as 4 feet (1.2 m). They need a very large, covered tank. Arowanas are jumpers and may leap out of an open aquarium. Arowanas live for as long as 20 years.

Arowana

XTREME FACT– A Singapore company was offered $80,000 for its rare "platinum arowana." It refused to sell its prized, pure-white fish.

LUNGFISH

Lungfish breathe using gills underwater, but they also have "lungs" that allow them to breathe air. The lungs are actually air bladders. In their native Africa, Australia, and South America, lungfish survive for months out of water when lakes dry up or turn to mud. Although they look like eels in water, these fish can move above ground using their jointed fins as "legs."

West African Lungfish

As pets, lungfish need an extremely large tank and a very committed owner. Lungfish can grow up to 6 feet (1.8 m) in length and can live up to 75 years. Lungfish are mostly lurkers who hide until it's feeding time. They are carnivores. They eat goldfish, shrimp, crayfish, and crabs. Some owners hand feed worms to their pet lungfish.

XTREME FACT – While it is possible to hold a lungfish out of the water, it will cause stress on the pet. It may twist around and try to bite what it thinks is a threat.

BETTAS

Bettas are also called Siamese fighting fish. If two male bettas are put in the same tank, they will fight. They are beautiful fish and popular pets. Bettas come in a rainbow of brilliant colors, including reds, blues, yellows, as well as black and white. They grow to about 3 inches (8 cm) in length.

Bettas are carnivores and eat other fish, shrimp, bloodworms, or betta fish food. They live for 3 to 4 years.

XTREME FACT – When two male bettas are released into a tank together, they peck at each other until one swims away. People gamble on which fish will be the winner.

OSCARS

Oscars are big fish with big personalities. They may pout when there are changes in their tanks. They may enthusiastically swim up to their owners, often recognizing the faces of people who feed them.

XTREME FACT– Owners who hand feed their oscars may find their fingers in their pets' big mouths. However, since oscars have teeth at the back of their throats, owners only risk getting nibbled.

Oscars grow up to 18 inches (46 cm) in length. They are omnivores, and have a reputation for eating just about anything that falls in their water. Oscars love to eat meat. They are often fed worms, crayfish, grasshoppers, and pieces of beef and chicken. They also like fruit, such as melons and oranges.

SALTWATER FISH

Saltwater fish are native to the world's seas and oceans. They live and breathe in a salty environment. Freshwater and saltwater fish cannot be kept in the same tank. Many aquarists fill their saltwater aquariums with the rocks and living plants that are native to their fishes's natural habitats.

PUFFER FISH

Puffer fish are unique. When scared, they suck in large amounts of water or air. This makes them double or triple in size into a big ball of spines.

Puffers often come to know the people who feed them their shrimp, crab, crayfish, and mussels. Puffers range in size from 3 inches (8 cm) to 2 feet (.6 m) in length. They may live up to 10 years.

XTREME FACT– Puffers have a deadly toxin in them. If eaten, it is usually fatal.

LIONFISH

L. ionfish are beautiful but dangerous pets for experienced aquarists. Each of their spines is filled with venom. They use the venom for defense. A sting on a human is very painful and may cause breathing problems, but is usually not deadly.

Lionfish use their camouflage and quickness to capture their prey of smaller fish and shrimp. They grow to about 15 inches (38 cm) in length and may live up to 15 years.

FROGFISH

The frogfish uses its dorsal fin like a fishing pole. On the end is an "esca" that looks like food to other fish and crustaceans. When the frogfish's prey is lured in close enough, the frogfish swallows it whole. There are about 50 species of frogfish. They range in size from 1-15 inches (3-38 cm).

XTREME FACT– A frogfish lives by itself in a tank. It eats other fish up to double its size. A frogfish can change its color and blend in with its surroundings. Fish may swim up to a frogfish, thinking it is a piece of coral or other plant. The frogfish sucks them into its mouth.

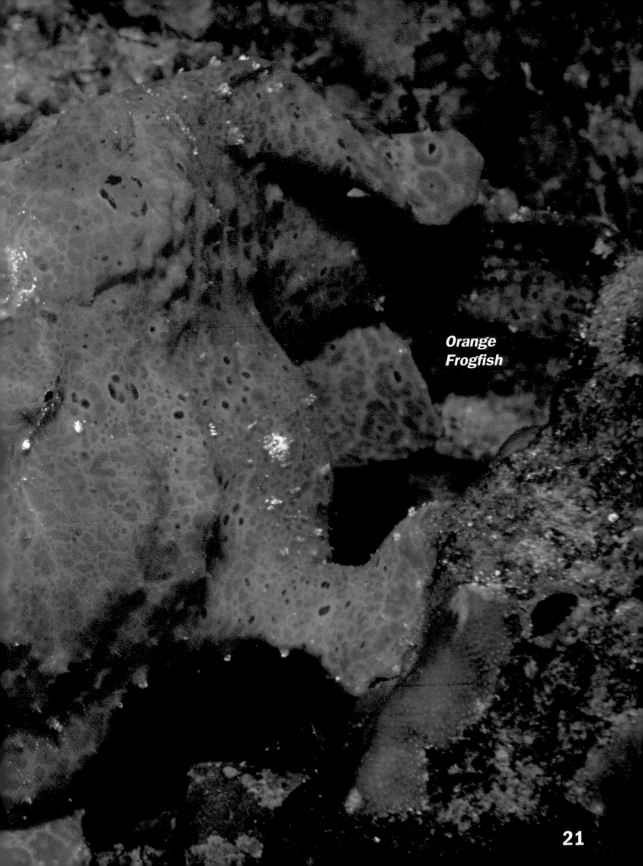

Orange
Frogfish

SEA DRAGONS

Sea dragons have amazing camouflage. Their bodies are shaped like the seaweed and kelp in their natural habitat in the waters off Australia. Some owners have to point out to visitors where their sea dragons are hiding in the tank!

Leafy Sea Dragon

Sea dragons grow 14-18 inches (36-46 cm) in length. They eat krill and mysida. They are sensitive fish pets, and need experienced aquarists to care for them. They were so in demand as pets in the 1990s, their numbers dropped fast. They became a protected species. Only captive-bred sea dragons are available as pets.

XTREME FACT–
Male sea dragons care for their mates's eggs in a special "brood patch" on the underside of their tails.

SHARKS

Sharks require huge aquariums in which to live. There are a few smaller shark species that make good pets. One is the epaulette shark. It grows to 30 inches (76 cm) and feels safe in confined spaces.

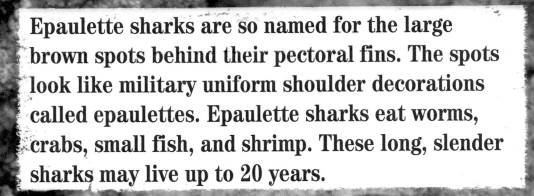

Epaulette sharks are so named for the large brown spots behind their pectoral fins. The spots look like military uniform shoulder decorations called epaulettes. Epaulette sharks eat worms, crabs, small fish, and shrimp. These long, slender sharks may live up to 20 years.

**Epaulette
Shark**

XTREME FACT – An epaulette shark is a "walking shark." Its muscular paired fins move in a way that makes it appear to "walk" across the aquarium floor, rather than swim.

MOON JELLYFISH

Moon jellyfish are easy to care for and make beautiful pets. They range in size from 2-15 inches (5-38 cm). Jellyfish eat brine shrimp or commercially bought frozen jellyfish food. Because moon jellyfish have see-through bodies, it is possible to watch their food moving from their tentacles up to their stomachs to be digested. Moon jellyfish live for about a year.

XTREME FACT –
Jellyfish need a special tank. If they are placed in a regular fish tank, the filtration system sucks them up. Today there are specially made jellyfish tanks that allow people to safely keep pet moon jellyfish.

Moon Jellyfish

POND FISH

Some fish owners keep large ponds in their backyards. They are stocked with large fish that need space in which to swim. Goldfish and nishikigoi (usually called "koi") are the most popular types of pond fish. They come in a multitude of colors. These fish often come to know their owners and are likely to swim up to greet them when it's dinner time.

XTREME FACT– The oldest koi fish was estimated to have lived for 226 years!

Koi

Koi are a Japanese carp. Typically, they grow to about 15 inches (38 cm) long and live for 20 to 30 years.

Koi are omnivores. They eat algae in their ponds, as well as worms, grapefruit, watermelon, lettuce, and commercial koi food.

GLOSSARY

CAMOUFLAGE
External coloring on a creature that allows it to blend in with its surroundings.

CAPTIVE-BRED
A creature that is not born in the wild.

CARNIVORE
A creature that eats meat in order to survive.

CRUSTACEANS
An animal with a hard shell and many jointed legs. Shrimp, crabs, lobsters, and crayfish are crustaceans.

DORSAL FIN
The fin that is located on the top of a fish's back. On a shark, for example, the dorsal fin is the one that sticks out of the water when the shark is swimming near the surface.

ESCA
The "lure" at the end of an angler fish's "illicium," or fishing pole. On a frogfish, the esca may be shaped like a worm, shrimp, or even other fish.

This lures in other fish who think they are about to eat their prey, but are instead eaten by the frogfish.

GILLS
Organs that allow fish to breathe underwater. Gills absorb oxygen from the water.

HABITAT
The natural home of a living thing. When owners recreate their pets's natural habitats, the animals live healthier, longer, and happier lives.

KRILL
Shrimp-like crustaceans. Many fish and certain whales eat krill.

MYSIDA
Shrimp-like crustaceans also known as opossum shrimp.

OMNIVORES
Creatures that eat both plants and animals as food.

SALTWATER TANK
An aquarium for sea and ocean fish with a salinity (salt content) of about 35 parts per thousand, the same as natural seawater.

VENOM
A poisonous liquid that may be used for killing or immobilizing prey, and for defense.

INDEX